Static

Joseph Duemer

For David Del Tredici —
thanks for your good humor &
high intelligence during the
interview — and before & after!

Owl Creek Press
1620 N. 45th St.
Seattle WA 98103

Acknowledgments

Grateful acknowledgment is made to the editors of the following publications for permission to reprint poems that originally appeared in them. Some of the poems have been revised since their first publication.

American Literary Review: "Van Gogh's Bed: A Love Letter," "Meditation on Bats"; *American Poetry Review:* "Theory of Tragedy"; *The Iowa Review:* "Sculpture Garden," "Dog Years," "Water Music"; *Manoa:* "Evening Air," "Dog Before the World," "What to Listen for in Music"; *Mississippi Valley Review:* "Air and Angels"; *New England Review:* "Sketch for an Elegy," "Plainsong," "Mathematics of Chaotic Systems"; *New Virginia Review:* "Walking as Prayer"; *North Dakota Quarterly:* "Pine,"; *Ploughshares:* "The Human Voice"; *Tampa Review:* "Reader Response"; *The Wallace Stevens Journal:* "Poem of this Climate"; *Yellow Silk: The Journal of Erotic Arts:* "General Semantics." Thanks to the Chester Jones and H.G. Roberts Foundations, as well as the *Southern California Anthology,* for recognizing, respectively, "Public Service Announcement," "Song: Notes Toward a Theory of Marriage," and "Superstition."

For support during 1992, I gratefully acknowledge a Creative Writing Fellowship from the National Endowment for the Arts. I also wish to thank the Corporation of Yaddo for a residency in 1991, and the Blue Mountain Center for a residency in 1992, both of which provided time to work on parts of this book. I am grateful to Clarkson University and its Faculty of Liberal Studies for annual Faculty Research Grants and for release time in the fall of 1990 and again in the spring of 1993, which supported my work on these poems.

The book's epigraph is from Robert Frost's poem "The Oven Bird." The title of the poem *Dog Before the World* is a translation of the title of a painting by the German Expressionist painter Franz Marc, *Hund vor der Welt* (1912). "Van Gogh's Bed: A Love Letter" contains a sentence from Iris Murdoch's *The Fire & The Sun.* The epigraph of "Reader Response," from Wolfgang Iser comes, I think, from "The Reading Process: a Phenomenological

Approach." The epigraph of "Walking as Prayer" is from Bruce Chatwin's *The Songlines*. The anecdote about Cardano in "Information Theory" is lifted from Jeremy Campbell's book *Grammatical Man*.

"Superstition" is dedicated to Claire Bateman; "Reader Response" to Robin Clark; "Plainsong" and "Sketch for an Elegy" to the memory of Evelyn Duemer; "Pine" to the memory of Craig Lindenberger; "Letter to My Anger" to Albert Goldbarth; "Air and Angels" to G. M. and Susan Osgood; "Van Gogh's Bed" to G. M.; "Sculpture Garden" and "Water Music" to Carole Mathey; "What to Listen for in Music" to David Rakowski, with sound effects; "Poem of this Climate" to John Serio; "Evening Air" to Michael Waters, thanks for the epigraph; and all three "Songs" are dedicated to Beth Wiemann, who set one. Finally, this book would not exist in anything like its present form without the friendship of Carol Frost.

Copyright © 1996 Joseph Duemer
Cover art copyright © 1996 Faye Serio
Cover design by Rich Ives

ISBN 0-937669-57-1

Table of Contents

Acknowledgments 2
Table of Contents 4

One

The Human Voice 10
Public Service Announcement 11
The Mathematics of Chaotic Systems 12
Music Theory: 1969 14
Evening Air 16
Sculpture Garden 17
Water Music 18
What to Listen for in Music 20
Song: Notes Toward a Theory of
    Marriage 22

Two

Pine 26
Sketch for an Elegy 28
Plainsong 29
Walking as Prayer 31

Three

Song: Notes Toward a Theory of Perception 34
A Meditation on Bats 35
General Semantics 37
Reader Response 38
Information Theory 41
Van Gogh's Bed: A Love Letter 43

Four

Song: The Chemistry of Common Things 48
Dog Before the World 49
Dog Years 51
Surplus Value 53
Letter to My Anger 54
Poem of this Climate 56

Five

Theory of Tragedy 60
Air and Angels 63
Superstition 67

for Donald Justice

The bird would cease and be as other birds
But that he knows in singing not to sing.
The question that he frames in all but words
Is what to make of a diminished thing.

                                      ROBERT FROST

One

The Human Voice

All night rain ran down the window
in the spare bedroom where I slept; outside,
the lime tree's runneled leaves absorbed
wave after wave of the Pacific storm,

which like a riot had been pre-
dicted by the authorities; awake
in the smallest hour, I heard
a woman's voice rise and join the weather—

my friends making love, their house
an instrument to amplify desire.
I wished them joy, marriage being
the hardest art I know of, and the least

certain of success. As I fell
asleep a voice rose from an alleyway
where I'd first heard it years before
in Fez, of a husband keening for his wife:

His fingers stroked the skin of dust
on the paving stones, ransacking their surface
for some comfort, knowing that
her body would be carried to the hills

it was just possible to see
from that place, where it would be laid beneath
the trees and sprinkled with lime,
to burn away the flesh. To sing.

Public Service Announcement

A modulated voice slides over the fade-out
of a sorry-I-got-drunk tune by Tom T. Hall.

There will be a benefit, it says, for a little
girl born last year sick with a disease so rare

it's hers alone, unique, a disfigurement
of nerves and tissue born of an intrinsic flaw

in the structure of the universe, a broken
symmetry at the very beginning of things

that gives rise to such spangles of dread
as only an afternoon of country music

at five bucks a head might benefit. The voice
quiets to a brief hiss of elegiac static

and another song begins, this one a maudlin
tale of ordinary pain and suffering, like this.

The Mathematics of Chaotic Systems

If weather systems can be described by mathematical equations that shift into chaotic behavior, then a change as slight as a butterfly flapping its wings near a weather station would make long-term weather predictions impossible.
                    IVARS PETERSON

The burly man on Santa Monica asks me
if I'd like to buy a rose:
"No thanks."
"Then do you know where I can get
a Kalisnikov with extra amunition?"

As he saunters toward the beach
I can hear the curved blue clips
coated with a fine sheen of lubricant
sliding into place with a satisfying click.
The life of the mind is a hard life.
In the soft evening light of California
each tight red rosebud
wrapped in a neat cone of shimmering plastic
glows like an angry coal
and leaves behind a wake of perfume
pungent as machine oil.

I remember trailing behind the Mexican girls
with corsages pinned above their breasts
outside the high school gym in San Leandro
and breathing in the sweetness
that loosened from their sweaters
while they danced.

I remember a few years later, breathing hard,
twisting and sweating
as I walked on glinting sidewalks, volatile
as alcohol, swinging my right fist
hard into my left palm
and imagining those faces I wanted
to pulverize, learning only slowly that anger
can be compressed into the curves
and stops of the singing voice.

But the man who hated everything
so much it silenced him
got himself a sheer black rifle
(shaped like a pornographic diagram of a woman's leg)
and set out for a school
where he got down on his knees in the dust
and started picking them off
like distant pigeons. Sunlight
glared from the white buildings so hard
he saw red everywhere,
but down the long blue barrel he watched his little
roses bloom on their chests and foreheads,
self-assured now as a sports announcer,
deadly as news.

Music Theory: 1969

Trying to stay awake because I love
the sheet floating like summer air
over my body I am letting go of
Sibelius' *Fifth Symphony,* allowing
the insistent pattern of notes to
dissolve in the silence above the bed.
Letting its rhetoric alone.

I love the music of getting in bed
with or without spouse or lover.

I love the radio's hiss
reminding me of space and time.

I remember who first insisted
I listen to the record, the argument
of her shoulders tilting me toward
attention. I wanted to kiss her.
Music, music, music. I want to stay
awake and listen to the house cooling—
joists and rafters popping, turning
the seven rooms into an instrument.

I love the instrument of memory,
balky and unreliable, hard to tune.

I don't give a shit for Stevens, who
owned the record (a scholar has averred)
and who never slept, to hear him talk.
The best dreams are waking dreams,
which fly like music into the mind.

The music grew steadily and
we watched the riot squad clean up
demonstrators in the street below,
the cops dumb percussionists.
That's music for you, hanging there
without a thing to do in this world.
Without a syllable in mind.

I love the body and the idea of the body;
I love music and the idea of music.

That's memory for you, swelling
like some stupid crescendo, like sex
or the memory of sex. Language
is violence, people outside the Century
getting the shit beat out of them.

Inside the complex lies the simple;
inside simplicity, complexities mount
into chaos, lately become a science,
and where authority is rhetoric.
Inside rhetoric, romance and silence.

In the heart of the world, I told her,
you are mine. Music, music, music.

I love the trees twenty years later
weighted with snow, insistent and brilliant.

I love the way memory becomes
a single point, one note from the score.

I love the vernacular silence
of hotel rooms, the eroticism of bad art.

I love bark peeling from birch trees
and the skin of my lover's wrist.

There are many things that cannot be
described but can be indicated, sung.

Evening Air

*You'll never know how great a kiss can feel
till you're stopped at the top of a ferris wheel.*
                            FREDDY CANNON

We waited, in summer twilight, to ride the ferris wheel
with yellow lights arranged in stars.
My moist ticket crumpled in my hand,
I wondered if I would be able to see clear to where we lived
on the edge of town, just barely inside
the dark blue steel of the tracks
catching the last edge of the sun. Across the fairgrounds,
a vendor hollered, his cry hanging
in the air faintly as a new star.
The stink of old marigolds rose from a little bed
near our feet, sweetened with cotton candy.
Standing beside you, waiting
to be taken up, I watched your breasts rise and fall
with each breath and I wondered how it was
going to feel to rise into the night
with you. The bar slammed shut across our laps and we
           were born
into a circuit of pleasure beyond our control:
looking down from the stars where we swung,
the dry bolts of our bench squeaking one small note over
           and over,
we knew none of those people down there
could tell us what to whisper
in each other's ears, so we began to make up a language
good enough to describe
(down to the shadows of eyelashes
lengthened by yellow incandescence across your cheeks)
our bodies, dependent on the lurch forward, the gentle
           rocking,
the wheeling machine of the heavens overhead.

Sculpture Garden

Crows break up the afternoon.
Their laughter is complete.
What do I care about?
I knew she would be my wife
when she ran her fingernail
along my arm as the orchastra
was beginning some slow
Mozart. The stars poured down
a parsimonious trembling
light, and we kissed leaning
against a mother and child
by Henry Moore, near a bird
by Calder, and a stainless tree
by David Smith. Who says
that art is dead? He must
answer to the muse's hardest
kiss. Let there be light.
The laughter of crows is
only a figure, a kind of
writing against this summer
sky, but it is convincing,
and as lovely as my wife's
breasts, which touched me
for the first time after
we were both bathed in Mozart.
Let there be dark.

Water Music

Gnats orbit my face as we float
on our backs in the brown river,
eyes closed or half-closed to the sun
and building thunderheads.
We are trying to recover our luck
by surrendering our bodies
to the current. A current runs
through everything, yes, but here
it is explicit—we are far
from the clean black beetles that do
authority's bidding, far from
the toxicity of bank loans.
All we have is this chaos in our hearts.
And water trickling over the mossy
lip of the dam down there as surely
as money, or love, making an inhuman
music on the jumbled rocks below.
A big turquoise dragonfly lights
on a floating twig, freezes: it
flexes its four wings so slowly
I fall further into the world
of dreaming. I think this may be
one of those rare moments of transcendence.
Don't you believe it. The dragonfly,
though beautiful, is as inhuman
as a jewel; its carapace is hard,
its eyes compound—it must see in clicks
and segments what we see
as smooth and round; a live mineral,
it needs this water to perpetuate
its ancient genes, which we do
on dry land, calling it by other names.
In love, we say, somehow
wrapping our brittle bones around
each other, swimming toward that music
neither of us understands. Music
like the jeweled clockwork

of the sun-drenched dragonfly's
four perfect wings that flex the light.
There is no secret in that light,
no matter how beautiful, how full.

What to Listen for in Music

Only that which is about to abandon the senses entirely
makes for pleasure: the summer sky at eight o'clock, thin

lavender washed above a line of oaks and maples that take
the light and turn it—what?—that turn it into sense.

So he finds himself driving through open farmland with his
    wife,
half-listening to a violin concerto on the radio.

The music sputters with a burst of static over Brahms—
the boiling cell of a thunderstorm passing east of the
    highway,

scuffing clouds of starlings from the fields, leaving
the air as lucid as last night's last dream, so much like life.

The solo instrument contests the orchestra, as convention
dictates, in a language not perfect but perfectly its own.

Rhythm precedes arithmetic; passion, true marriage.
    There
is no present moment untroubled by the wash of memory,
    a sequence

of minor chords struggling against the morality of the
    tonic.
The problem is how to carry rhythm and passion into
    institutions

like mathematics and civil law designed specifically to curb
desire. The music seems to come from *the world itself.*

Coda: The earliest concertos harmonized warring
    instruments;
only later, after the Self got capitalized and went into
    business—

swaggering with pride in its ontology—did the soloist step
forward from the body of the orchestra with the intention
    of saying

something in particular. Something that required assent.
So he knows there is no language fitted exactly to that
    light

slanting into the wall of trees at the field's far edge, that
    marriage
is a conventional art. And having found himself thus alive

under the massive push and pull of weather, which follows
    rules
of its own devising, and is indifferent to assent, he begins
    again

to understand desire, and what to listen for in music—that
    which
until now has existed only in the silences that enclose each
    note.

Song: Notes Toward a Theory of Marriage

I became dizzy in my own house. Going up
and coming down the stairs, dizzy.
Standing at the top or at the bottom,

the world swayed. I couldn't make sense
of objects floating before me—there were
no words for them, though they gave off

an odor like ozone after a lightning strike.
Things pulsed. Stroked. Then a morning
when the house was filled with light,

but nothing glowed deeply. Surfaces
once polished splintered and gave way to dust,
as if we lived at the heart of an accelerator

designed to reduce things to their
constituent particles. The kitchen gods
transformed themselves to mere appliances—

useful, but also safe from our maneuvers
of resentment. Our things were only things,
no longer the famous things-in-themselves

we'd begun with. Everything began to drop
from our hands: a plastic bottle of seltzer
a china saucer scissors the coffee pot

the phone on which we might have called for help—
each strict object making a distinctive sound,
the signature of its damage, by which we

might know it, broken or whole. Those were
the most exciting days of the marriage.
Though we still believed in the metaphysics

of accident, not fate, we were learning to love
the explosions of milk cartons; mail flew
from our hands—magazines and bills spun

to the floor where the dogs walked on them,
making a salad of pages paw-smudged
with mud from the river. So when she fell

at my feet, tripped by something invisible
in the weave of the carpet, it was natural—
I didn't recognize the genius of this perfected

gesture until later that night when in a storm
huge limbs cracked from the pine and lay
sprawled in the driveway. I wish I had a sense

of form, the ability to juggle the objects
of experience that whistle through the rooms
of the house. The smooth contours of things

fractured. The wind calmed and the moon, heavy
with history, arced across the bedroom window,
placid and truthful, falling slowly toward us.

Two

Pine

    The morning rainy enough
that even the small birds are quiet
around the feeder hanging
from a pine bough in the yard.

The old pine is beautiful
with its deeply fissured bark
        and its green needles
darkened by the steady fall of rain.

The sap flows from cut branches
        and crystalizes. This is not
blood, and we will be wise if
we distrust such easy metaphors.

My friend is dead across this
trampled continent, and an old lover,
now a beautiful young mother,
        mourns him, and his failure.

    The dog loves light rain
and wet grass that glosses the fur
        to his ankles, making
the fine structure of his bones

apparent. My friend's heart
stopped in the middle of an empty
gesture. I hope to be more like this
        dog, without any gestures

and I love the bloody world, its trees
juicy with sap and its sparrows
        that know when to shut up.
I am only capable of mourning with

        the definite article,
which whispers like a pencil working
sums that prove the emptiness
        of elementary particles.

The pine tree's bark is streaked
white and glows in this flat light
    of early morning.
      I can smell the pitch

when I step out the back door
    and go across the wet field
to my honest job. My feet sink in.
The day is good, my friend dead.

Sketch for an Elegy

After the last snow has melted, thick
shadows of cumulus move across my yard,
and the stiff green fans of new iris leaves
unfold in the wind as precisely as tools.
The air must be almost as cold as this river
polished by spring sunlight
where my dog swims hard, white legs igniting
the black water twisting beneath him.
These granite boulders in the river
must weigh almost as much as the bruised clouds
overhead, whose shadows flatten against
the rippled surface of the water.

The body, of course, is mostly water.
On the morning of her death my mother
would have watched the iridescent faces
of grackles turn toward her from their perches
on pliant branches beyond her bedroom window—
birds sketched in negative space, voices whining
with desire, as beautiful as bruises.
On her table would have glowed gaudy irises
taller than my father. The body that suffered
my birth would have been the same body drowned
by the slow, cold current of its cancer.
Here is the dog emerging from the river.

Plainsong
My townspeople what are you thinking of?
              WILLIAM CARLOS WILLIAMS

         1.
When my mother died I had nothing to say.
She believed in the originality of sin—in these

last year's leaves driven tumbling along the curb
of Sunrise Way (her last suburban address—

the streets in this place domesticated
with subdivision names, graveyard latinized

to cemetery, which the management calls—god
damn them—a memorial park). We buried her

to the prattling of a fool, a hireling
who mispronounced our family's name, degrading

even the small sincerities of platitudes and flowers.

         2.
This place is serviced by two freeways
and a major arterial for easy access. Easy to find

as the Ford dealership. Spring sunlight slanted
down and I slipped a tag of Dickinson's

I'd written out into the flocked pine box
(built on the same chintzy lines as the tract houses

she occupied all her married life.) I don't
believe in God, or in that fancy paradise

shaped like a wedding cake most of the family
still hold on to, but I know the sacred when I see it:

the plain plaid dress my father chose—
blue with thin red lines, something

she might have worn around the house on Sunday
after church, covered by an apron while she cooked.

It is the meals we take that make us holy, if anything—
the smell of cooking. All through the service

a dog barked beyond the fence, the sound muffled
by the wind washing through the trees.

    3.
She told me once in church I couldn't carry
a tune in a bucket. Said it was all right, though—

she couldn't either. I wouldn't have expected her
to understand how beautiful I found that insistent racket

the dog made, so unlike sobbing. Her life was unhappy
because she believed creation was imperfect, the heart

filled with lies, depression and anxiety, needing
to be beaten down with belief in something better.

She never liked my music. There is nothing better.
The heart, if not creation, is imperfect.

    4.
I stand beneath the wheeling trees. High summer now.
The stone with her name settling in the ground.

The rhetoric of grief is microtonal, a kind of droning
chant like the background static of a vivid dream

that stays with you all day long, a reminder.
I stand beneath the wheeling trees adrift in light.

What am I waiting for? I begin to sing. It doesn't matter.

Walking as Prayer

Sluggish and sedentary peoples, such as the Ancient Egyptians—with their concept of the afterlife journey through the Field of Reeds—project on to the next world the journeys they failed to make in this one.
                              BRUCE CHATWIN

1.
He is a skinnybones in red windbreaker
and he walks around the village all day long

at an aerobic rate. I mean around
the village, on the outer roads, loop after loop,

a wraith or scarecrow driven by the daemonic
wind of every season. This must be prayer. Instead

of dropping to his knees, he bends them, pushing
forward one energetic genuflection at a time.

Above his head the willows leaf and fill
with wind. A phoebe hovers by the creek, its call

a counterpoint of prayer—closer to the mark, I think,
because less desperate. After dark

my headlights sweep across his back, though he must
eventually go in somewhere. Lie down. Rest.

2.
This one steps carefully along the sidewalks
glittering in sun, where students have the night before

chucked cans and bottles in the gutters. Dressed
in a hard-pressed suit, and with steel-gray hair

combed neatly back (each tooth-track showing), he shows
the red face and exact gestures of an alcoholic; he does

not want to be eccentric, so he picks the cans
and bottles up for their deposits using nothing

but his fingertips to put them in his plastic bag so
that he doesn't soil his cuff. He doesn't look

at anyone, and I'm not sure if he's ashamed. Is he
a blessed man engaged in rituals that slide away

from sense and circumstance? Does his reverence find
each night what he's been praying for all day?

      3.
I stand at the window as mottled light slides
through neglected apple trees, so that I see

my own unsettled face reflected in uneven glass.
I need to walk, skirting the built-up edge

of the village, where the smell of french fries
mixes with the faint breath of iodine

from the Emergency Room. Two starlings skirl, building
a nest for the second time this season beneath

the disconnected drainpipe of an empty house.
The glassy taste in my mouth is fear. Yesterday,

out here, a kestrel unfolded the air and took
a lazy, glossy, perfectly innocent pigeon in mid-coo.

I've walked this far trying to believe in God
and found these feathers drifted across the field.

Three

Song: Notes Toward a Theory of Perception

It takes an effort of imagination
to hear music, or even voices, in this
water coursing over cold granite boulders

as round and heavy as planets.
Let the river stand for everything
we'll never understand. Perception

is seduction: a woman and man undress
in a room in a city neither of them knows—
They have never felt anything like this before.

It is easy to slip into those spaces
between the cloudy probabilities
of matter. Their bodies

pump out rock & roll—they are making
the story again about this world
as the species sees it, certain

wavelengths of light making sense,
the rest a welter of invisibles. Their sweat
leaves angels on the snowy sheets,

which stretch away for acres
in all the directions of curved space.
That was beautiful, the woman says,

inventing aesthetics;
You ain't seen nothing yet, says the man,
inventing the blues.

A Meditation on Bats

They wait for those late evenings in early Spring
when the light goes limpid and the air just chills.

They must sense that early insects, improvident, as in the
　　　Fable
of Selection, drugged with cold, will be easy sonar marks.

In summer they will be all over the place, swooping
through the branches that dip almost to the surface of the
　　　river.

In summer, yes, they will flutter around the streetlight
at the end of our road, feeding richly on moths, which have

their own phenomenal world of images to contend with.
Tonight, as the shadows of the maples are erased by
　　　darkness,

bats come across the mirrored water, emerging from the
　　　broken
windows and ruined chimney of the farmhouse on the
　　　farther bank.

Naturally, if humans hadn't been here three hundred
　　　years
they'd be coming from a cave. Out of some natural feature.

Deep in the woods even a rationalist feels on the verge
of falling into some grim narrative centuries deep—

there, in crevices in the rocks you can almost see them
curled in the shadows, hearts barely beating. We can only
　　　imagine

their faces, they go so fast through the pools of light
in the yard beneath our windows: just as their high songs

are inaudible, so their live bodies are invisible.
A leaf-shape will swerve into sight, not fast, exactly, but
　　　nimble

and a little warmer than anything else with wings. All
        poems
about bats are the same poem. We would like them to be
        more

like us, but in any true taxonomy bats will be grouped with
        snakes
and sharks, who, going about their regular business in the
        world,

are most dangerous in our frantic minds. Who don't fog
        their sharp
senses with language. Whose fables are four-dimensional.

All dreams are the same dream and the imagination is an
        old house
with a broken spine, a dark body full of inhuman thought.

General Semantics

I loll, I loll, all Tongue
  THEODORE ROETHKE

As I understand it, Korzybski, freezing,
shuddered through the First World War deep
in the trenches. Who can blame him for wanting
language made rational and just, purged

of uncertainty? It ought to be easy to scrub
metaphor from our sentences, to excise the copula
to be from the structure of Thought. Then
maybe we wouldn't find so many ways to lie.

But we crave transgression like salt.
To sin is to invent again what it means, being
human. Adam and Eve, after all, finally understood
on that evening, everything they had been saying.

The body, at least, delights in thresholds,
recovering the taste of innocence in bed
with the wrong lover. Illicit and polymorphously
perverse, dear, our language longs for paradise.

Reader Response

If reading removes the subject-object division that
    constitutes
all perception, it follows that the reader will be "occupied"
by the thoughts of the author, and these in their turn will
    cause
the drawing of new "boundaries."
                      WOLFGANG ISER

Be patient that I address you in a poem,
    there is no other
        fit medium.
The mind
    lives there.
                  WILLIAM CARLOS WILLIAMS

    How can he ask her to help
him read this? What would it mean to ask her?
    There is no telling what she
would find herself saying if he found the nerve
    to ask her to untangle
the grammar he uses to patch his dreams into
    semblances of waking
sentences. He would like to draw her, dear reader,
    nearer and nearer—until
she would fall into his grid of dialects as if
    they were real places—
for instance, a room filled with a pattern of shadows
    and yellow light, fat
pillows and a tremendous bed, an old comforter
    flung at its foot, and flowers—
big sweet ones the color of honey. He would die
    just to watch her
untangle her hair and unclasp the devices securing
    her clothing secretly
to her moving body. (This reader is a dancing god.)
    He has of course prepared
for this, religiously shaping a single sentence
    in which the small seeds
of comfort bloom from the soil of each word, turning
    the intimate fire beneath her skin
into the perfect fulfillment of his temptations,
    red as apple skin.
Impossible, he knows: words never touch literal

                    flesh, not even the least
tip of the seeking tongue engaged in glossolalia
                    or cunnilingus. He feels
the force of this paradox, knowing it is all he is
                    likely to feel:
He can only ask for her help with this matter
                    if she first approaches
willingly, without his making the slightest motion
                    in her direction.
Only then might he ask for her help—after syntax
                    had already lifted from them
like souls from the cold bodies of the dead, when
                    every possible grammar
has drained from their muscles, loosening their
                    bones into the sweet,
almost incomprehensible slang of sex. Then he might
                    ask her—when she
leaned against him half drunk on his language
                    as pure and primal
and perfect as the day before the Lord knocked
                    down Babel.
Then he might ask her, as they lay loosely together
                    after love's precise positions
had relaxed, propped against big pillows, the light
                    spilling across her breasts
casting insouciant blue shadows as still as fish
                    sunning themselves in tropical
shallows. Every abstraction, he knows, wants a body.
                    Still, he is filled with
the stillness of authorial guile—he only wants her
                    to respond, after all, to use
her vivid imagination. He wants her to sing
                    a song as certain
and dry as a contract or a canzone—a Renaissance
                    dream of words
perfectly aligned, capable of flying to the ear
                    of the beloved,
whispering like sweet wine in the throat.
                    He wants her
to read him like a book of her own choosing,
                    La Vita Nuova,
about a man for whom desire is its own reward, a

          boundary where the world opens
on a mist of light, a place in the mind where the body
          finds comfort
and a little peace, a place like that in which the figure
          of the patron appears
inconspicuously in the corner of a sacred painting,
          where it will not harm
the composition, a gentle jest at no one's expense.

Information Theory

There is no perfect knowledge. Happy endings?
    highly improbable:
There is an infinity of tragic futures to choose
    from, but only one
you want. The noisy gizmo at the science museum
    drops hundreds of white
balls randomly through a field of pegs, clattering
    so the gulls rise
from the reflecting pool and wheel over the grounds.
    The balls come to rest,
settling into a lovely bell curve, a mountain
    conceived wholly
in imagination, that could not exist in the here
    and now of the eroded
moment where we live on the surface of landscape
    carved by contingency
and microclimate. In the long run—as luck would
    have it—things find
shapely forms—those raw mountains regular as waves
    if we could look at them
through long pulses of geologic time. Good luck.
    Fat chance. Lecturing
the physicist admitted science is not about truth
    but pleasure and elegance
which are not the same as beauty, which is always
    messy, washing its hands
in the world. Gerolamo Cardano, inveterate gambler,
    bless his heart,
was thrown in 1526 from his carriage—a lone die
    from the croupier's cup—
and later that year after losing badly at primero
    then falling into a canal,
disgusted with himself, wrote *Liber De Ludo Aleae,*
    a little handbook
about games of chance, inventing the theory
    of probability. So he was
the first to calculate our chances for happiness:
    disaster after disaster,
unhappiness without end. Still human optimism

                    desires knowledge
of the improbable event that might loosen us
          from the easy
habit of acceptance. For the improbable to have a chance
          someone has to give
the ratcheting machine a swift kick so that one ball
          skitters sideways
against probability, to fall in love with loneliness,
          communicating its bit of
information—its mad difference amid the necessary
          redundancy of things.
Everyone knows there is a ghost in the machine;
          what no one knows
is how to put such gauzy vapor to useful work
          in the world.
Will the lovers find courage to leave their marriages
          for the jazz of New Orleans?
Will they manage to improvise a singular moment
          against the momentum of
everything else, separate from the wash of moments?
          Will they develop
a consistent theory of the Self? What if they do?
          Will they find themselves filled
at last with sufficient and necessary information?
          And what will they know
then without question? Nothing they don't know now
          poor things.

Van Gogh's Bed: A Love Letter

God creates the original Form or Idea of bed. The carpenter makes the bed we sleep upon. The painter copies the bed from one point of view. He is thus at three removes from reality. He does not understand the bed. . . .
　　　　　　　　　　　IRIS MURDOCH, paraphrasing Plato

Dear—— Van Gogh's earliest drawings—he came late to
　　　genius—are skewed
and awkward, his line scrubbed with erasure. He blames
　　　only himself.

Drawing as understanding, a frantic charting to confirm
　　　appearance—
to collaborate with the world's changing light. The
　　　windows tense.

But the world had changed in the middle of the previous
　　　century—
something had twitched in history and the molecules of
　　　matter filling

the universe now for the first time shuddered under the
　　　impact of sunlight.
When Van Gogh tries to sleep the sound of rain fills his
　　　mind.

When he is able to dream he dreams of something called
　　　the solar wind.
Awake, he struggles with the fiction of perspective, his
　　　senses

working to register their excitement, his brain a
　　　photovoltaic cell
pulsing with power. He knows the world matters more
　　　than himself.

The workman's shoes, tinged with blue, are impossibly
distant, but the nipple, deeply red, of the reclining nude,
　　　comes forward. Both explain themselves.

So many millions of words shifting uneasily in a thousand
   libraries,
all of them shaped into monographs explaining how red
   and green

vibrate in his paintings: *The Night Café,* floor tilted up
   into
a stage with the billiards table like a bed in the middle that
   the man

and woman leaning into each other at the back table might
   lie down
on, and *A Room at Arles* with Van Gogh's own bed, its
   blanket turned back

and pillow breathing a little in the sunlight—so much
   grammar for a man
nobody talked about in his life, and so many sentences,
   that nothing

can dissolve the echo of misunderstanding. A painter I love
   has accepted
that she might not be able to sustain her work, which costs

money and requires an audience. She knows no one may be
   interested
in her gift. Or the idea of painting as a gift. Or the idea of
   seeing clearly.

I wish I lived in a tiny country torn by civil war, with a
   small and difficult
language. I would whisper in such a language into the
   pillow on the small,

unwieldy bed in the corner of her studio. Only outside the
   body could we
know the final forms of things, and we could not live
   outside the body!

Rain falls into the industrial streets as it fell into those
 corn fields;
the crows of Brooklyn are the same crows—maybe—as
 those black check marks

of Saint-Rémy echoing from the nineteenth century. All
 the light we need
floods everything, darling. Plato, apparently, loved the
 darkness of authority;

Language itself, spoken, is already bad enough; paint
 committed to a surface.
Van Gogh made his narrow and difficult bed for us to lie
 down in.

We understand the bed. It is our duty to think hard about
 what we are doing
and what the world's hot and cold surfaces mean to us.
 Without irony. Yours——

Four

Song: The Chemistry of Common Things

Schumann heard a single tone,
the concertmaster's pure A,
drone inside his head—background

radiation against which angels sang
the songs that moved the world.
There was also hell. He believed

in hell because he had to, hearing
his century's sinners groan.
All of it was music to his ears.

Sounds gnawed at him like a rat
in the wall: a prodigious mathematician,
he had to turn them over in his mind—

imagine the way stones feel
to the stream washing over them,
how water feels to the stones,

all of it flickering between
what the eye sees and what the mind
knows to be true. The idea that

singing angels move the planets and grasp
suffering isn't hard to understand—forces
in the world must come from somewhere.

But such music is an empty set, pure
information humming with the energy
of everything else—in raw earth

molecules of silicone shifting
into quartz, singing the sine
wave that lifted Schumann from the world.

Dog Before the World

Our dogs observe the yard: patchy
lawn, apple trees in blossom, pine
and cedar—they take it all in
in shades of gray, though scent must
detail the world for them as color
does for us. Two purple finches
shoot straight up—flight almost vertical—
to the top of the house
and perch there on the gutter singing
or whatever you want to call it.
Yesterday a shy gray phoebe took
the same post—after hovering a moment
in mid-air—then made for the thick
pines, from which he began
his two note call. But now
the finches are going at it like crazy
and it is sex of course
they are discussing. Some would have it
that bird genes are singing
(or whatever you want to call it)
amplified by delicate bodies
and the curve of copper gutter.
Our big dogs ignore the little birds,
hearing as well as seeing, apparently
in shades of gray. This
give and take may be genetic
though I don't like the idea—
its implications do not flatter those
who think our songs are songs, that
the voices chirping in our throats
as we walk along might somehow belong
to us; that the fricatives of sex might
tell a kind of truth—fantastic hope!—
about the larger world. The truth
of the matter hovers as it must
(like the phoebe, carefully
picking insects out of air)
between the magnificent and formal Self
if that's what you want to call it

and the astounding sunlit garden—
a world I can see from here, complex
beyond belief. An intricate crochet
of molecules impells the birds and unfolds
flowers out of thin air. I understand that
but stand dumbstruck nevertheless
attentive at the window, shoulders
slightly hunched—innocent, almost,
as our dogs before the world.

Dog Years

Well, in a hundred years when
an army of blind crows scratches
with scarred claws in the duff
at the edge of the browning woods
by the river; when new grasses
tough as knotted rope have grown
that have never heard
the historical whisper of languages
and the religions spawned thereby;
when old trout burn
huge and muscular near the bottom
of the drunken river from which lush
weeds coil;
            when no hammer blows
fall like cold syllables in the heart
of the village to ring the Spring air
and prick up the ears of old dogs
sweltering on our porches;
when our dogs twitch their fine noses
at the acrid combinations
of leaf smoke and the cold burnings
of fungus;
            when it is all over
for us, even in this rural paradise
of conservative voters; when
dropped by an atrophied arm
the stainless steel pot clatters
to the kitchen floor, and long after
the ritual of mail delivery
has ceased its comforting
punctuation, and after the fine ash
of incinerated trash has filmed
the school windows—those who
have strength will push open their doors
and send out their suffering dogs,
who will glance nervously
over their shoulders as they descend
the sagging porch steps beside
the basket of curling geraniums,

wagging their tails in the wan hope
characteristic of their species
(so long accustomed to the sound
of our languages over their heads)
but who will begin soon to fend
for themselves, to form a better government
a more perfect union, a pure code
constructed of growls, more suited
to the world of accelerated mutation
that will be their inheritance.
To forget us will take them
less than a generation.

Surplus Value

It is a privilege the lecturer said to work
with our minds instead of our backs. But I envy
those old farmers standing outside Smiley's this
morning, their faces stained leather, leaning
with their boys against the fenders of pickups.

The speaker meant to tell how lucky we are to spend
our working days bathed in jittery illumination,
and I know what she meant. My mother's father,
who grew alfalfa and corn in harsh light
was nothing like an American agricultural saint.

Married late—after a life at sea—he beat
his children with a strop; it would be sentimental
to report he also read them Shakespeare and the Bible.
Once he had a vision in his irrigated valley
of a wall of water sweeping a whole town away.

To wake next morning to news of flood beyond
the dry San Gabriels. Vision is a kind of work, I guess.
But it's hard to imagine the boys outside the cafe—
the sons of the pioneers—engaging their minds this way.
Country music rattles from their broken speakers.

It is our responsibility she said to speak the truth.
But I'm not sure I believe any longer in the pure
clear word. A clutch grinds, a fender bangs
a bumper. Mine or yours? The sharp edges of this
world break into song. And not just birds.

They're mostly assholes, naturally, chucking empties
along the road. Weekends they squabble in the bars
over the ownership of women. They don't believe in art.
Their laughter breaks like static over the morning's
birdsong. Call it a privilege, the birds say, to sing.

Letter to My Anger

Dear Anger. I've got a lot of questions. Multivalent
questions about the chemistry of your body, which
has the power to effortlessly inhabit my body. Which
makes me think your body is my body, the fit is so
lovely. So are you some kind of cheap space alien who
needs a way to breathe earth's atmosphere, your home-

world bathed in methane and ammonia, stinky and volatile
gasses likely to explode? Do you need me, Anger, as
much as I need you? Where do you come from? That's
what I ask myself when I find myself—find myself, do
you hear?—slapping the dog because she wants to go
one way and I want to go another. Sometimes, god help

me, it feels good to hurt another thing. Is that all
you're up to? Are you trying to hurt me, make me sick?
I feel sick after you flash through me—a hangover
nausea that makes the air smell like literal shit, scats
and droppings the hound pulls toward in the woods,
      wanting
to get her nose right down on top of that electricity,

which, I've read is a million times stronger to her
than to me. Are you an alien, then, with nefarious chem-
istry? Or do you belong to me, a sort of black sheep
guardian angel, the shadow of an angel? A *them,* or simply
me? For a long time I've believed you are an abstraction
called moral failing, but I think now that

you may be a moral feeling. But what good are you?
Let me phrase that differently. What possible function
do you serve? What situation on the ancient savannah bent
my ancestors' chromosomes into your nasty shape? Did
      you
make the body stronger, pumping adrenaline laced with
endorphins into chimp bloodstreams, eliciting the murder-

ous, highly effective scream? Well, you're no longer
needed: we go to the polls these days, unless it's a matter
of religious hatred or ethnic identity, unless you have
given us good Reason. Or maybe, in spite of the slaughter,
you do us good in other ways? Do you give us new
        thoughts?
Do the tsunamis you unleash make new structures

in consciousness? Perhaps you are the secret father
of genius. Or do you just like a good fight, my Anger?
So you show up like Black Jack Davey seducing the
        master's
young wife. Do you feed on emotions like those invisible
beings in that old *Star Trek* episode? You erase thought,
galling the nerves with static. You don't make snese.

As far as I can tell you leave the animals alone, belonging
to my species as surely as mathematics. Perhaps you are
the fractal root of chaos, all those jagged demons
jittering in the brain during an argument. My dogs, though
they can be lonely and have their feelings hurt, are never
angry. What kind of ghost are you? The ghost that loves it-

self, you enter the houses of the long-married, sending
your mice into the corners to ruin the bread and leave shit
like little seeds; you rattle the dishes in the night.
Are you ever righteous? Didn't you fill old Amos up, who
railed against the sins of Israel gone soft and politically
corrupt? Do you ever do the work of the gods? It's hardly

a syllable between a thing and a being. Here in the world
I'm less and less certain I can tell the difference. I want
to caress what swims and sings through my field of vision,
        not
slap it into obedience. But there are stellar moments, dear
Anger, when you sharpen the edges of everything—objects
and thoughts about objects. In closing, then, I remain
        yours.

Poem of this Climate

The heads of those peonies sway
slightly in the late afternoon
light—deeply red
blurs floating in a slanting corner
of the yard. One single iris
rises there, its manifold face
open for anyone to see.

In my heart's backwardness
the women I've thought loveliest
have been a little dowdy
and pinched around their eyes,
faces entirely without
guile, though a little too long
or too round. They have
swayed me beyond measure
in uneven light.

The perfectly pretty—those
with nothing ungainly
to conceal—need no unbuttoning;
they must regret nothing. Everything
is already there to be seen:
slim irises rising
among awkward peonies.

In rooms reached by sagging stairs
in renovated houses,
I talked half the night.
The reluctantly unhooked dresses
and loosened breasts
were not some little prize,
but the empirical kiss
the world sometimes relinquishes.

So I believe in love, though
less now than before—I have stood
before mirrors as uneven
as a lake's windswept surface,
and bathed in the amber

light glinting from figurines
and bottles of cologne
while from their beds with flowered
sheets (covered
with dusty sleeping bags)
they have fixed me
with contracted irises, knowing me
superfluous
to the deepest purposes
but necessary, too, like a Christian
angel, an agent of some Will
greater than the future
tense. I have felt the light
shift, as if a storm had passed
at dawn, leaving the sky perfectly clear
and set with only a few shreds
of white cloud like discarded clothing.

The pure peonies sway
in a light so perfectly uttered
it cannot be countenanced
and the intricately sexual
parsings of a robin's song
drift through the open window
on the white air of morning.

Five

Theory of Tragedy
How can we believe in anything again?
                        ECHECRATES, in *The Phaedo*

Why didn't the first philosopher want to go on living
among the sun-warmed stones of his native city?
Wasn't the music, microtonal as sunlight on paving stones,
worthy of him? Didn't he have friends
whose particular talk he loved more than the cool beauty
of ideas? There was as yet no definition of tragedy.

His students say the old man believed deeply
in the clarifying power of disputation, urging them
that argument leads always toward truth, though
it never arrive There. He loved to form definitions,
        believing
them like music, for which, apparently, he had no ear.
There was as yet no definition of tragedy

though everyone knew what he or she meant by the
        word—
a certain feeling in the bowel
as you filed from the theater after something by Sophocles,
a bristling of hairs on the small of the neck, evidence
of poison working out toward the skin,
the body politic purging itself of doubt, bending

its confident demotic beneath the weight of music
and dance. But out in the streets Socrates heard the
        passion
of speech slide into Rhetoric, which was invented, some
        say,
in order to contain the passions roused
in the populace by the music of speech.
There was, as yet, no definition of tragedy.

Was Socrates so sold on himself he couldn't imagine
(the whisper of god in his hairy old ear)
the fine words of those citizens talking among themselves
on the marble steps of the King Archon's palace?
He thought they were dangerous, tugged this way and that
like a tide destroying the walls of the city.

The rationalist philosopher Sherlock Holmes loved
to play music when not testing blood
stains on a carpet—scratching away like crazy at his
     violin—
a fine old instrument better than his skill—making music
the more terrible for its awful Victorian sentiment.
The problem of tragedy is how close it always must come

to sentiment. Both these philosophers hated democracy—
the dirty feet of the mob, the bumbling stupidity
of the man in the street, who loves the fat that sticks to his
     own bones
and therefore is no fit audience for tragedy. Tonight
as I read, the faint odor of skunk drifts through the
     window.
I imagine the dogs of Athens raising their noses

into an ancient breeze off the Aegean carrying the sour
     smell
of the philosopher's corpse after he has accepted poison
from the jury of citizens. Would the private eye, so adept
at uncovering what others called tragedy, have been able to
     determine
the cause of death by examining the famous scene in the
     prison?
And had the first detective sniffed out the hemlock

would he have deduced the fibers of the soul floating loose
in the damp air of the cell? What would he have thought
of the crooked smile on the round gray face?
And what analysis could have made the tears smearing the
     faces
of those wealthy and self-sufficient men gathered there
in the prison yield useful knowledge?

The outer stones of the prison, already warmed
by morning sun, and the city's air vibrant with music
     rising
from its streets, the shopkeepers sold fish, copper, fresh
     bread,
and the red figure ware common to that place and time,
     often

depicting Clytemnestra's bloody betrayal of Agamemnon
or famous episodes in Odysseus' long journey back

to his wife—both impossible fictions! The dogs might have
made some music with those old bones, even lacking
a theory of tragedy, which is really a theory of knowledge.
Tonight, odor of skunk hanging like a philosopher's soul
in the air, I sit beneath a xerox copy of a photograph—one
     of those
Greek vases called a lekythos, this one showing a daughter
     of Memory

loosely draped, feet bare, sexy, her right hand indicating
a songbird on a branch sketched near her knees.
Without a definition of tragedy, we cannot understand
the dance our words and grammar pattern intersecting
the facts of the palpable world—a maple tree's black
branches against the amber/blue stripes of sunset,

perfume of skunk and wood smoke hanging in the air.
The old man always said his wisdom was nothing but
     ignorance,
and at the end of his life he couldn't prove the soul
survives the body. Perhaps it was nothing but a feeling,
like tragedy, which is only the awkward singing
of a small bird on a flimsy branch pointing toward
     memory.

Air and Angels

It is a langorous evening in Eden.
      Light fades
from the quilted river and the first
      persons' sense
of self fades like that ancient light.
      How well they know
their minds are empty! That's the price
      God exacts
for walking with him in the evening.
      The air cools
and a fine dew appears on the leaves.
      The closer
He comes—strolling fluently among
      the million trees
of the garden—the less they know: His
      is a voice that
turns out in the end to be utterly
      intolerable.
It is a langorous evening in Eden. Yes.
      The flickering
celestial swords come later, writing
      their refusals
in the air of the garden by main force.
      Those angels' job
was to carve heaven from the firmament:
      the first Rational
Act in the world, slicing the innocent
      ecosystem pulsing
through the garden where nothing ever
      happened into parts,
called knowledge. That was the price
      of being God's
sad, wild, disobedient children. Sin
      was strange
and new, a first act of imagination.
      So there is a lyric
silence everywhere, like God, or his first
      absence. Or that
perfect fold of late sunlight coruscating

                the surface
of the Tigris. The tongue is a devil.
                Name the animals,
God said, and after that there was science
                everywhere,
and faith's niggling curlicues. Now
                I begin
to understand my father, an engineer
                who designed
golden screws tightened inside the lathed
                ceramic nosecones
latched atop ballistic missels in the 1950s.
                Everything
looked the same to him, and he believed
                in a God who
wanted him, each Saturday of my early
                adolescence, to humble
himself by volunteering to janitor Grace
                Brethren Church.
At evening he'd come get me from the pool
                of our apartment block,
where I'd have slid my hand inside
                a girlfriend's suit,
our slippage broken by the troubled surface
                and mottled light
of the blue chlorinated water (stirred
                by healing angels?)
where we treaded water. Adam and Eve
                would have been so happy
until that moment of anguish in which they
                learned to work.
We worked like hell in God's house
                polishing linoleum
in the sanctuary (which looked for all
                the world
like an expanded version of our split-
                level living room).
The old Romans were astonished—having
                pushed their way,
swords flashing, past the priests,
                to find the Holy
of Holies dead empty. Grace depends then

        on sin's richness.
I'd take along my radio—Ali had stopped
        Liston—and listen
through cement static to rock stations
        applying solvents
to the fixtures in the house of God.
        Certain Christians
show devotion by dancing with rattlesnakes
        deep in the pines,
their piety proving itself by risking
        a wild metaphor
rooted deep in Eden. We did not believe
        in anything
as wild as metaphor—the only language
        we trusted
was the inerrant KJV translation printed
        on onionskin that
rustled each Sunday like summer leaves
        in a light wind.
Mostly engineers and programmers with brittle
        spirits in need
of beautiful sentences, our church accepted
        only the glossolalia
of ionized particles whining through space,
        insisting this
was God's voice whispering in the garden.
        Interested,
I watched the trees of high summer waver
        through the sanctuary's
frosted windows. Presented the choice
        between science
and faith, I chose faith in physical science.
        Saturday before
I'd discovered objective evidence of the
        World's Body—cleaning
the toilet in the Ladies Room I found
        a blond pubic hair,
making me forever an Empiricist. Grace
        finds multiple
expression here in the world—my father's
        fervent baritone
(now I can say it) rising above the mumble

   of the congregation
and/or the inadequate sign language my hands
   might make shaped
by breasts my fingers curled into an alphabet
   that names something
sacred—or make themselves otherwise useful
   in this world.

Superstition

Walk forty-seven mile of barbwire,
Use a cobra snake for a necktie,
I got a brand new house on the roadside,
Made from rattlesnake hide.
I got a brand new chimney made on top
Made out of a human skull . . .
Now come on take a little walk with me,
Now tell me, Who do you love?
Who do you love? Who do you love?
                                        BO DIDDLEY

At noon the upright human body casts
           no shadow,
or the shadow is driven straight down
           into the body.
Sharp grass blades and fat stones disappear
           in glare.
The road shimmers and puddles with black
           light in the distance.
The Romans believed ghosts struck at noon,
           explosions
of white-hot sunlight flaring out from
           the base of a wall,
a white column flayed in light. Disaster
           always
takes place outside the hot, slow pulse
           of the world,
and boredom, which casts no shadow, uncoils
           at midday,
among the tumbling demons of light, so
           they believed.
Jesus must have found the man who lived
           among the tombs
trembling and naked at noon, bleeding
           and chained,
cowering in the brilliant Mediterranean
           air. And when
he cast them out with a white stare, the devils
           screwed themselves
into the swaying bellies of nearby swine,
           who pitched
into the sea. And when a sane man staggered

>   into town that
> afternoon, only the old men remembered him.
>   In the dead air
> of these suburbs, sunlight is smashing
>   the sidewalk slowly
> to grit, making the blurry music of noon
>   that no one
> wants to hear. The fretting baby quiets,
>   seeming to hold
> her breath so long her mother hurries
>   to the crib
> to see what is the matter. A young man
>   with the flat stare
> and autistic sneer of criminal authority
>   pauses, robbing a store
> by the highway, to lift a quart of beer
>   from the cooler—
> rolling the cool bottle over his forehead,
>   he notices
> the spastic flies trapped behind the plastic
>   beer sign,
> where, also, a little blood is spattered
>   like punctuation.
> The girl waiting in the car will be glad,
>   he thinks,
> for his thoughtfulness. He checks
>   his reflection
> in the glass door going out, waves back
>   his hair
> with his hand, a gesture a little like
>   a salute.
> A compressor hums out back—one low note—
>   and ghosts
> flicker in the dust kicked up by trucks.
>   At noon
> the maenads tore young Pentheus apart,
>   says Euripides—
> during the stalled momentum and sexual
>   panic of midday. Later,
> as rain dripped quietly into the cistern,
>   they were very sorry.
> For an instant the young housewife is glad

>   her child is dead,
> and she dreams—the windows burning at noon—
>   of passionate travel
> to romantic islands. The baby coughs
>   and squalls
> in the heat and she lifts it from the crib,
>   smoothing
> its damp hair and cooing her gratitude—
>   she will be able
> to keep thinking of herself as herself.
>   Tiresias, in wide hat
> strolls the sidewalk and scowls at the
>   cool windows
> of the houses. A husband coming home
>   passes his wife's
> lover coming toward him in traffic, singing
>   with the radio.
> Who do you love? Who do you love?
>   The song rough
> with static. A detective is collecting
>   evidence:
> the store's air conditioning is on—
>   heat flows
> from the clerk's cheek into the cold
>   linoleum,
> doing no useful work—one more example
>   of general
> disorder, molecules smashed to weightless
>   subatomic
> particles in the center of the sun
>   and streaming
> through what we think of as the substance
>   of the earth.